THE RISE AND FALL OF CT PLUS YORKSHIRE

ALEX CLOUGH

AMBERLEY

First published 2024

Amberley Publishing
The Hill, Stroud
Gloucestershire, GL5 4EP

www.amberley-books.com

ISBN 978 1 3981 1899 7 (print)
ISBN 978 1 3981 1900 0 (ebook)

British Library Cataloguing in Publication Data.
A catalogue record for this book is available from the British Library.

Origination by Amberley Publishing.
Printed in the UK.

Introduction

Starting in London in 2001 under the Hackney Community Transport name, CT Plus first went north in 2006 when the company won a number of Metro MyBus contracts in Leeds and the surrounding districts. At first they operated these from a small base near Geldard Road to the south of the city. As this began to grow, a small operation began in Hull, using a number of ex-Dublin Volvo Olympians on school work and BMC Condors on a newly won Park & Ride tender from the city to nearby Priory Park. This Hull operation was very short-lived and closed around half a decade after it opened. The Olympians were sold on and a number of the BMC Condors transferred to Leeds and Wakefield.

The main part of the business would see its first major growth in 2015 when the West Yorkshire business purchased a fleet of four Dennis Trident Plaxton President buses for newly gained double-deck school contracts. The vehicles were purchased new by First London and had been converted to single door and repainted yellow at the EnsignBus dealership. The vehicles received white 'CT Plus' branding that they would carry till the end of the business seven years later. Alongside the purchase of these Dennis Tridents, the company developed a strong relationship with local dealerships and gained a variety of other double-decker buses. These buses were used on the school contract services that they had gained from the closure of Geldards Coaches in September 2015. Through this a number of vehicles arrived, primarily ex-London, with a fleet of X, V and W plates as the most common. Most of these buses operated in service in white; however, the small fleet of three 'V-LGC' B7TL ALX400s, new to London General, received similar company branding as the Dennis Tridents with yellow stickers over their white paint. In anticipation of continued growth at this point, the Leeds base moved to a larger site in Holbeck, which was closer to the city centre.

As the Leeds operation gained a variety of double-deckers for work, the Wakefield business also got their taste of these, with buses regularly transferred between the two depots as required. Maintenance work for the West Yorkshire business was undertaken at two locations, one north and one south of Leeds city centre, so buses would be seen commuting between the two places frequently. The next big leap for CT Plus would be the shrinking down of the M Travel operation in Castleford during 2016, which saw the company gain their first full fare-paying public service work. Previously, the business had operated the Dewsbury Free Bus service for a short period of time. It would get its first taste of further-afield stage-carriage work by winning the tender for the weekday 183 service between Wakefield, Castleford and Pontefract. At the time, CT Plus won a small number of peak-time workings that required a single bus with M Travel continuing to operate the service during the main daytime. For these workings, the initial choice of bus was ex-Hull Park & Ride BMC Condors, which were painted white and carried roll blinds. The roll blinds were quickly replaced by LED boards. Following this, in April 2017, M Travel had their O licence revoked and, although they carried on under the Stanley Gath name for a short time after, initially gave up some tendered work. Some of the services that were given up included the 39 and 49 routes in Pontefract that CT Plus gained and operated out of the Wakefield depot. These routes operated six days a week and began by using the BMC Condors; however, double-deckers regularly appeared on this work too. When the Stanley Gath business fully collapsed, CT Plus was the main operator to step in on a number of their school contracts, using recently transferred Dennis Tridents from HCT London that arrived at the start of April. These buses operated in London red throughout their life in Yorkshire and would never be painted. Service contracts continued to be added and although the Dewsbury Free Bus service was lost to Yorkshire Tiger, the school business continued to grow. During 2017, CT Plus Yorkshire launched the short-lived 'Join Book Drive' minibus scheme across east Leeds and this could be seen as setting up the region for the Flexibus network now in the area. The scheme, based at the Leeds depot, used a fleet of sixteen-seater minibuses, which were stored at a number of community centre locations and could be hired out by groups at any time. Drivers were trained at CT Plus and could also drive school bus services when not hiring a minibus. Unfortunately, this scheme did not last long, with most of the trained drivers transferred onto full-time work in the company.

In July 2018, the CT Plus business saw further large expansion when the group agreed to purchase Hellaby-based independent Powell's Bus, which saw the operator enter South Yorkshire. Powell's Bus was a deregulation-era operator that ran a mix of local service and school contract work with a fleet primarily consisting of ageing Dennis Darts, Tridents and Volvo coaches. Upon takeover, the Dennis Darts were quickly replaced with Optare Solos from Blackpool Transport and Enviro200 buses from local dealerships. Elderly coaches were temporarily replaced by newer coaches before the decision was made to withdraw the type from the fleet following the loss of some new college contracts that they were used on. As buses were replaced, a large number of withdrawn buses began to appear at the Leeds depot and were either used as spares donors or were awaiting further sale. As they were already present in the fleet, it was decided to retain the Dennis Tridents in this business, which consisted of ALX400s and East Lancs bodied, the latter purchased from HCT Group London by Powell's Bus a year before the buyout. The takeover of Powell's Bus by HCT Group saw a change in direction for the business with a focus on local service work in areas not previously served by the operator. Shortly into the takeover, Powell's Bus won a large amount of local contract work in Sheffield from Sheffield Community Transport and over time trialled ideas such as increasing their peak-time X7 service to operate from the city throughout the day. This was sadly short-lived.

With continued growth in Leeds, mass batch purchases of double-deck buses began to take place, with a group of fifteen ex-Go Ahead London B7TL Geminis arriving in 2018 and eighteen ex-Lothian examples of the type arriving during mid-2019, the latter including three that were based at the Powell's business to replace some withdrawn Tridents. The ex-Lothian vehicles arrived to assist on established contracts as Metro began to close the MyBus contract that saw them take back their leased BMC Condors and auction them off. CT Plus kept a small number of these that they directly purchased; however, the majority were returned to Metro and replaced by double-deck buses. As these upgrades were taking place, the Wakefield depot gained the 113 hospital bus contract linking Dewsbury, Wakefield and Pontefract hospitals using the M62 motorway. The contract required two vehicles and to start with three Bristol Community Transport Enviro200s were diverted on order for use on this contract. These were quickly replaced by another three Enviro200s that replaced the diverted ones back to Bristol. By July 2019, the Leeds depot had begun operating regular public service work after winning the Horsforth town bus 30 from Fourways, which gave up the contract to focus on their private-hire business. The Leeds depot also began operating the 61 service in south Leeds and the 81 between Pudsey and Leeds to replace a section of the First Bus 11 service in Leeds that had been separated. This saw the true beginning of Enviro200s in West Yorkshire with the arrival of a bunch of Enviro200 buses that were then replaced by MMC variants a short time later.

The Leeds base continued to trial concepts at the time, with one ill-fated idea in the form of Vamooz, a concept that was to make school services easier to use and utilise the buses on hire work at weekends. The bus that was repainted in the purple livery was Volvo B7TL X587 EGK – it spent a long time in unbranded purple before receiving Vamooz names mid-2019. Unfortunately, by the time the branding was applied, the concept had been abandoned due to the lack of private hires. The bus would continue in this livery in service until it was withdrawn a year before closure due to a low bridge incident.

March 2020 saw the arrival of the Covid-19 pandemic and CT Plus continued with their service work in a reduced format in line with the guidelines issued by the government during this period. As things began to calm and people were able to travel further again, some services that had been suspended during the lockdowns were reinstated. During lockdown it had been agreed that Transdev would purchase the Flying Tiger business, which ran the service to Leeds Bradford Airport; however, as this was taking place, Flying Tiger was unable to reinstate the Leeds to Airport 757 service when restrictions eased. CT Plus stepped in and purchased two 2011-plated Enviro200s to operate this service on a temporary basis from June till August 2020, with an hourly frequency and limited evening service due to the lack of demand for the route at the time. Despite the short-term nature of this contract, it was decided to create special branding to reflect the use of these buses on the 757 with the name 'Runway' used on the side of the vehicles. As initially announced, the contract ended at the end of August and the two Enviro200 buses transferred to the Powell's business, where they helped to continue the fleet upgrade and contract gains there.

Before the start of the Covid-19 pandemic, HCT Group announced the closure of the Manchester Community Transport business and this eventually folded in April 2020. This was a business that was very short-lived in HCT Group ownership owing to complications with Transport for Greater Manchester and financial troubles. Upon the closure of this business, a number of newer vehicles continued with CT Plus Yorkshire and were used to further standardise the fleet used in public service.

To balance out the closure of MCT in Manchester, in summer 2020 CT Plus gained a number of local contracts in Huddersfield from TLC Travel, which prompted the opening of the Brighouse depot to cater for this work. With the influx of new contracts, CT Plus was forced to operate services when the depot wasn't ready, with buses having a dead run to and from Leeds daily. When the depot was finally ready, it operated with a caravan as an office within the yard. The yard had previously served as a base for the now closed Red Arrow Coaches and as storage for withdrawn buses from the closed Yorkshire Greenline operation. The services in Huddersfield were colour-coded for a short time and the launch of the services saw a paper book published that featured all the times and a large network map inside.

Later in 2020, Powell's Bus became a contracted provider of Sheffield Supertram replacement bus services, operating on the long-term Halfway to Sheffield Blue Line closure for a short period and the Middlewood to Sheffield Yellow Line closure during weekends in September. For this a variety of buses were used, with many for the Yellow Line replacements consisting of ex-Lothian Gemini buses on loan from the Leeds depot. Around this time, Powell's Bus also introduced the new 117 service following demand by locals. This service connects Bramley and Rotherham in between school times on weekdays and is still operated to this day despite the demise of the company.

Powell's Bus had expanded even further by spring 2021 with the award of the contract for a new connecting Park & Ride service for Doncaster Hospital to ease a parking issue on site. The Park & Ride site is located next to Doncaster Racecourse with a five-minute trip by bus to the hospital entrance. The operator initially intended to use a Scania double-deck bus on the service; however, with the contract including a requirement for a newer bus, the purchase of a Streetdeck double-decker was made. This Daimler-engined bus was new in 2018 and arrived from Arriva London, which sold it early in life due to it being non-standard in their fleet with its HEV configuration. The bus in turn received appropriate branding and operated this service, minus involvement in an RTC and requiring a rebuild, until the end of the business. Although growth was still taking place, it was apparent at this time that gaps were beginning to widen in parts of the operation. With a repaint programme taking place and new 'ivy' branding applied to many buses, some vehicles missed out, with a number of the ex-Go Ahead London Geminis either operating in white or still in their London red livery. Paper blinds were also becoming more common, with maintenance issues at Brighouse resulting in unsuitable minibuses substituting for broken Enviro200s on service.

Despite this, further growth hit CT Plus Yorkshire in summer 2021 when an agreement was struck with First West Yorkshire to operate a number of their services whilst they reversed a nationwide driver shortage that had hit First heavily. The services were operated by CT Plus on behalf of First West Yorkshire with CT Plus providing the buses and the drivers whilst accepting First Bus tickets. This initially began in June, with Leeds depot starting to operate The Springs X26 and X27 services alongside the Leeds, Seacroft and Cross Gates service 11. These were later joined, in late autumn, by First Halifax services 539 to Stainland and 587 to Rochdale which had new Enviro200 MMC buses specifically brought in for them. The Leeds service began by using Enviro200 MMC single-deck buses; however, due to capacity issues on the spring services, these were converted to double-deckers for the most part. This contract work lasted until early 2022 when First West Yorkshire returned to operating the services.

So where did CT Plus stand by spring 2022? Following the loss of the previously mentioned services back to First West Yorkshire, the Enviro200 MMC buses brought in for the Halifax routes were used to upgrade the mix of older counterparts used on services operated by Wakefield depot. The Wakefield depot by this point had changed its service work slightly to introduce a number of peak morning trips to reduce dead mileage, gained a singular round trip on a local Arriva-operated service in Castleford and had standardised the 39 and 49 services by combining them into one route. As the year progressed, the newer buses brought in to help Wakefield depot attempted to create a better image for the company; however, they worked slow to achieve this. As a consequence, they lost a large number of school contracts in the area to Arriva mid-term, as well as the Pontefract bus service work in July to Globe Holidays, which was growing in the area. Whilst this was occurring, Leeds had purchased four ex-Tower Transit London Volvo B9TL Gemini 2 buses to support their school contracts in the city. These vehicles ran their lives at the company in London red and without proper destination displays. Things had stabilised for the most part at Brighouse; however, at Powell's Bus a number of old school bus Tridents were gained from Wakefield and pressed into use alongside other tired members of the fleet. At this point it was a regular occurrence to see a Powell's bus in service with a paper destination blind and 'broken bell' paper notices became a common feature aboard.

With all this considered, it came as no shock when on Tuesday 2 August HCT Group announced the closure of the CT Plus Yorkshire and Powell's businesses, citing financial troubles. Rumours circulated that the company had amassed a large amount of debt and had the intention of closing all operations the following Tuesday. This plan was short-lived as by Wednesday it became apparent things would close on the Sunday; however, on Friday morning at 6 a.m. a notice went out that by 5 p.m. that day all operations would cease. As the company was a CIC business it voluntary brought in administrators, who arrived around mid-afternoon to close down the business. The last week saw a big change in how the business functioned, with all double-deck buses withdrawn in favour of single-deck buses on all services. On the last day itself many buses were missing from diagrams as drivers had not shown up for their shifts due to lack of confirmation that they were going to be paid. At 3 p.m., a notice went out for all buses to return to depot with people abandoned along routes and buses arriving at the depot in convoy. It would take South Yorkshire PTE and Metro West Yorkshire until the following Monday to reinstate any of the services.

Until the influx of double-deck buses, the main buses in use by CT Plus Yorkshire until 2015 were a strong fleet of PTE-owned BMC Condor vehicles leased to the operator for their school contracts. One of these, YK55 GRT, is seen here between duties in East Leeds.

The scale of these vehicles at the Holbeck base in Leeds can be put into proportion with this line-up of four examples of varying ages awaiting the afternoon school output.

Awaiting the afternoon school bus run, Dennis Trident Plaxton President LK03 NLA and a sister vehicle wait to start their trips in north Leeds.

The Holbeck depot in Leeds was also responsible for the citywide AccessBus contract work with a range of dedicated drivers and vehicles for this. One such vehicle is YJ09 KZZ, seen here operating a service in North Allerton.

Although the fleet was predominantly newer 2009-plated Solos, CT Plus retained two of the first-generation low-floor Solos purchased for this work. X168 NWR is seen here in its later days about to operate an afternoon AccessBus contract local to the depot.

Having a short break on its way back from a morning north Leeds school service is Dennis Trident Plaxton President LK03 NKS.

The smaller Wakefield depot regularly shared buses with the Leeds operation to cover for fleet requirements. Volvo B7TL Plaxton President W452 WGH is seen at the Wakefield depot prior to a transfer run to Leeds in return for a BMC Condor.

An unusual bus retained by Metro and handed to CT Plus for AccessBus work was YJ07 HER, a longer-length Optare Solo new for Leeds Free City Bus work operated by First Leeds. The bus was refurbished inside with extra wheelchair spaces for AccessBus work.

One of the newest BMC Condor vehicles operated by CT Plus was YK10 AVV. This was one of a small number owned by CT Plus that were new to their Hull operation for Park & Ride work. It is seen here in Leeds depot prior to operating its dedicated school run.

Complementing X168 NWR on the AccessBus fleet was X172 NWR. Due to a considerable number of faults this vehicle was withdrawn in 2017 and lingered in the depot for a long period after this before donating parts and being scrapped.

Some of the first larger contract work gained was the Cocoon Festival shuttle-bus work between Leeds and nearby Temple Newsam. Seen at the latter terminus is Volvo B7TL Plaxton President X149 FBB.

Upon winning the Dewsbury Free Bus contract, Dennis Dart MPD MM51 XVB was acquired and operated this route alongside a short-lasting Wright Streetlite and an ex-London Dart. It is seen here at Leeds during its period on a dedicated school run.

In March 2017, CT Plus Yorkshire was offered six Dennis Trident Millennium-bodied vehicles from HCT Group London to assist with the increasing number of double-deck school services. HTL 5 and 9 are seen at Holbeck depot just after arriving.

Sister vehicle HTL 6 was parked opposite these. Once prepared, these Tridents would spend most of their eventful lives at Wakefield depot with only a small number ever painted out of the London red they arrived in.

As festival work continued to expand, a line-up of buses is seen at a site near Wetherby whilst taking driver breaks between Mint Festival shuttle-bus work. This was the biggest festival CT Plus Yorkshire would run with every serviceable double-deck used.

Volvo B7TL ALX400 V113 LGC, one of three of this batch in the fleet, is seen on Sovereign Street whilst blinded up for Cocoon in the Park shuttle work.

Mint Festival work required the use of staff and vehicles from the entire operation at the time, with Wakefield buses also ending up on the shuttles. HTL 3 is seen at the Mint Festival site.

Earlier in the day, HTL 1 is seen leading a line-up of London red Dennis Tridents from Wakefield depot on the morning of Mint Festival. At this point, these buses had been in use with CT Plus Yorkshire for less than six months.

Seen loading punters for the busy Mint Festival in 2017 was, at the time, Leeds-based LK03 NLC, featuring a 'Festival' banner to denote the work they were being used on. These banners were only used for this particular year.

On occasion the Wakefield-dedicated ex-HCT Dennis Tridents would be placed on loan to Leeds depot to satisfy fleet requirements. HTL 6 is seen here whilst on loan to Leeds operating the 2017 Cocoon in the Park shuttle service.

During the 2017 school year, CT Plus operated a number of MyBus school contracts that were further afield from Leeds. One such run was the TS1 that operated from Titus Salt School in Saltaire, Bradford. BMC Condor YJ56 ZTF is seen here waiting to start the route.

Seen operating back to depot following completion of its afternoon school run on the S56 service is BMC Condor YK56 EEA. This was one of the first repainted to feature a green swoop instead of red to represent exhaust emission work that had been undertaken.

On occasion, the oddity vehicles on fleet would appear as cover at times of dedicated MyBus BMC Condor shortages. One such working was BX54 DLK, an ex-HCT Group London Dennis Dart, seen here after completing the S56 school service.

Following contract losses by M Travel, Wakefield depot became the first part of the Yorkshire operation to begin public service operation with peak-time 183 trips. BMC Condor FJ59 UYE is seen here leaving Castleford bus station on the first afternoon trip to Wakefield.

Although traditional roll blinds were sourced, the closure of M Travel a short time after resulted in Wakefield depot gaining more routes, with the BMC Condors given LED blinds for these. FJ59 UYE is seen here again, this time in Hemsworth on the 30 service.

As the service work expansion continued in Wakefield, the depot also gained operation of the NHS shuttle bus 113 from Tetley's Coaches. With the short-term nature of the takeover, new buses were loaned from Bristol, such as Enviro200 YX17 NSU.

It did not take long before the odd double-decker appeared on the new public bus services. A regular for a period was LED-blind-fitted Dennis Trident LK03 GGJ, seen here leaving Wakefield bus station on its return trip to Xscape.

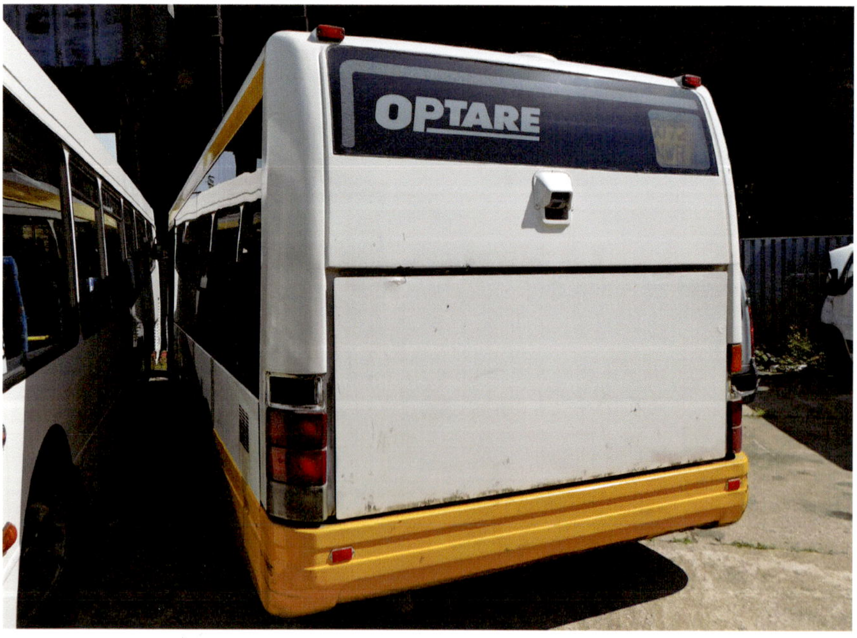

After lingering in the yard for some time, X172 NWR was finally moved to the scrap corner to donate parts before it was sent for scrap. On this visit the bus was being stripped for parts kindly donated to a locally preserved example.

The small number of ex-Hull Park & Ride BMC Condors owned by CT Plus became regular workhorses on their public service work. FJ59 UYK is seen arriving into Pontefract bus station after a trip from Hemsworth.

Seen making an unusual appearance on the evening 183 service during its short period at Wakefield depot is Volvo B7TL ALX400 V113 LGC.

At the end of summer 2017, CT Plus Yorkshire gained a large number of 2002-plated Volvo B7TL Geminis from Go Ahead London. Seen shortly after arrival is LF52 ZSF at the Leeds depot awaiting preparation for service.

Once the first arrived – LF52 ZRR, seen here – these vehicles made appearances in Leeds depot in mass and were prepared for service with a quick turnaround prior to the imminent start of the new school year.

As a Christmas present of sorts, December 2017 saw the arrival of the first brand-new buses for CT Plus Yorkshire in the form of three short Enviro200 MMC buses for the 113 NHS shuttle bus. SN67 XBJ/K are seen here shortly after delivery.

It did not take long for these vehicles to enter service, and the following month SN67 XBL is seen at Dewsbury District Hospital before a run back to Pontefract via Wakefield Pinderfields Hospital.

In the new year, the last remaining older-generation Solo on AccessBus work was withdrawn in the form of X168 NWR. Here it is seen at the back of Holbeck after suffering a failure that was not be fixed. The bus was sold for scrap shortly after.

In 2018 the real launch of the 'Join Book Drive' scheme, worked on by CT Plus Yorkshire the previous year, took place. This scheme enabled community groups to borrow vehicles, such as WJ65 BOF, for use in the local area. The scheme was discontinued a year later.

Over at the Wakefield depot the influx of double-deck school buses on public service work continued. Volvo B7TL ALX400 V120 LGC is seen here arriving into Pontefract bus station.

For a period, Wakefield depot gained some of the ex-London Geminis to help with operation requirements. LF52 ZTH is seen here on the 49 circular service. Note the LED destination blind that was applied to all these vehicles upon preparation for use.

In 2018 CT Plus Yorkshire made a big step south with the takeover of South Yorkshire independent Powell's Bus. Before the takeover Dennis Dart X93 FOR was seen at their Hellaby depot whilst on an enthusiasts tour.

Around the time of takeover, newly acquired ex-Blackpool Transport Optare Solo YJ08 PFF was seen in the Rotherham bus station operating a 4 to Ravensfield.

Upon the Powell's Bus takeover, CT Plus did not hesitate to introduce a fleet upgrade programme to replace most of the elderly fleet. One such vehicle introduced to replace older buses was YR59 NPF, seen departing Doncaster Frenchgate.

The Wakefield depot continued to prosper in 2018 with the award of the 485 service from Arriva Yorkshire. At this time, the depot began to introduce Enviro200s onto local work, with ex-HCT London YX63 DHC seen leaving Wakefield bus station.

Alongside the purchased Enviro200s for the 485 and to upgrade other services, a number of these buses arrived on short-term loan to cover others been prepared for use. MK63 XAC is seen here fresh from its loan to First South Yorkshire earlier in the year.

With a major focus on fleet upgrades, a number of BMC Condors and Optare Solo YJ07 EHR are seen in the withdrawn corner at Leeds depot awaiting major work due to significant faults.

Above and below: Although operation expansion was a good thing at the time, disaster struck with the first major incident at CT Plus Yorkshire with the writing off of HTL 5 due to an engine fire. This vehicle was operating Mint Festival contracts and on an empty trip to Leeds caught fire shortly after exiting the M1 motorway. Unsurprisingly, this bus was not rebuilt and was subsequently scrapped. This was only the first thermal incident for this batch of ex-HCT London buses.

With the high rate of expansion taking place at Wakefield, the depot was treated to more buses that became dedicated there until the end. These were in the form of three ex-Lothian Dennis Tridents, one of which, SN04 AED, is seen parked in the depot.

The lack of maintenance facilities within CT Plus Yorkshire resulted in broken bus corners emerging in depots. Seen in such a corner at Wakefield depot is Dennis Trident LK03 GGJ with an unknown fault that required it to be placed on blocks.

At the end of 2018, the relationship with NHS contracts grew with the gain of this work in Doncaster. Enviro200 MMC YX68 URG was acquired for this work and is seen at Wakefield. Due to contract agreements, this work could not run from the Powell's business.

Seen during its short time in the withdrawn corner is YJ07 EHR looking very sorry for itself minus all its rear lights. Due to it being owned by Metro, this bus was rebuilt shortly after and saw use on contract work until the end of the operation.

Volvo B7TL Plaxton President W447 WGH was one of the many random and leased double-deckers that arrived to assist on school work. Here it is seen returning to depot after its afternoon school run.

A very random transfer in 2018 for a short period of time was WV minibus SN08 EHD, which arrived from the Bristol operation. This vehicle was at Leeds depot for a brief time before leaving the fleet.

A long-standing member of the minibus fleet that left in 2018 was Ford Transit HN05 KJF, which was branded up for the short-term 'Leeds Alternative Travel'.

Continuing with the theme of rather random minibuses, LDV NK07 CYL made a short-term appearance at the Leeds depot in 2018, sporting separately painted wheels and MyBus school-related branding.

Initially used as a vehicle for the short-lived 'Leeds Alternative Travel' work, Renault car RX07 LCY lived out its last days as a staff transfer car before being sold.

In 2019 Leeds depot gained their first public service contract in the form of the Horsforth town service 30 from Fourways Coaches. Enviro200 SK15 GXZ is seen in Pudsey on a weekday extended trip. This bus only operated with the company for a few weeks.

As the minibus replacement continued, unique vehicles such as this tri-axle VW minibus arrived from HCT London. YX57 BHJ was one of two that arrived and were used as spares for AccessBus and school work when required.

In 2019 CT Plus Yorkshire saw their largest single batch of vehicles purchased in the form of eighteen longer-length Volvo B7TL Geminis from Lothian buses. These 2005- and 2006-plated buses are seen here shortly after arrival at Leeds depot.

The Volvo B7TL Geminis from Lothian arrived in fully decommissioned format at CT Plus Yorkshire with most pressed into service in this condition after the addition of ticket machines.

A further odd addition at the time that was utilised on AccessBus work whilst existing Optare Solos had emission upgrades was YX10 AYF, another minibus transferred from HCT London.

One of the first ex-Lothian B7TL Gemini double-deckers pressed into service was SN55 BOF. This was used in as acquired condition and is seen here in between school swimming bath shuttles in north Leeds.

CT Plus began to apply their livery and branding to buses in the Powell's fleet with the gain of a number of local Sheffield contracts previously operated by Sheffield Community Transport. A new acquisition for these was ex-Malta Optare Solo SR KX14 FHH.

With their prominence on school contract work in Leeds, CT Plus teamed up with Vamooz in the hope that the scheme would expand. To support the short-lived nationwide scheme was Volvo B7TL X587 EGK.

A surprise vehicle to appear at the CT Plus Leeds depot was Dennis Trident ALX400 KN52 NEF, provided by a leasing company as a short-term loan. This vehicle did not remain with the company long and only appeared on school services.

Above and below: Just before the end of the academic year in 2019 disaster struck in the form of another vehicle fire at CT Plus, this time involving one of the Metro-leased buses. BMC Condor YJ56 ZTL was travelling along the Leeds Inner Ring Road when the engine burst into flames. Following extensive damage, the vehicle lingered in the Leeds depot for some time before it was scrapped.

As newer vehicles began to arrive, more of the Powell's Bus existing fleet was withdrawn. Volvo B10M coach R24 POW is seen at the Leeds depot after being withdrawn from service.

Another small expansion was the introduction of the 81 service between Pudsey and Leeds to replace the First Bus 11, which was cut back. YX17 NTU is seen operating on this service, serving areas previously covered by Yorkshire Tiger, Geldards and First.

Updates to Powell's Bus also used existing Yorkshire buses such as Dennis Dart BX54 DLK. Previously featured in this book in London red, it was painted for use at the Powell's operation, in turn replacing older examples of the type.

A vehicle introduced at the time of the takeover which updated the fleet was VDL SB120 Cadet YJ55 KZT. This replaced a similarly liveried Dennis Trident on the Parkgate shuttle bus when demand reduced due to the introduction of a charge to use it.

Over the Pennines in Manchester, HCT Group purchased operator Manchester Community Transport during 2019. This was a short-lived operation with YX19 ONR, seen here at a bus rally. This vehicle would go on to serve with CT Plus Yorkshire shortly after.

One of the vehicles that was inherited with the HCT Group takeover of MCT was Dennis Dart MPD EU06 KNR. It is seen here on a Rochdale local service, one of a number the operator ran on evenings only. This bus was sold on after the MCT closure.

With a Powell's Bus paper blind and blue fleet number, Dennis Dart MM51 XVB is seen here out of use in the withdrawn corner of Leeds depot in its de-branded Metro Free City Bus livery. Shortly after this photo was taken this bus was withdrawn.

Seen adorning the CT Plus 'ivy' livery is Optare Solo SR KX14 FHH, which was newly acquired at the time. It is seen here with fleet number 6 shortly before a regional fleet numbering scheme was introduced that saw these in the 1800 series.

After many years with fixed blinds, Metro began to fit their leased Optare Solo buses with LED blinds for multiple uses. Two examples are seen here departing the Leeds depot, one heading onto AccessBus work and the other on a school service.

During the Covid-19 pandemic, CT Plus operated essential school contracts using buses with reduced capacity. Ex-Go Ahead Volvo B7TL LF52 ZSR is seen heading out to operate a Cardinal Heenan contract with a vastly reduced capacity of fifteen passengers.

During the Covid-19 pandemic, CT Plus also continued to operate their range of local bus services for those who required the use of them. Seen on its way to Pudsey is Enviro200 Midi YX65 RHU, operating one of the weekdays only extensions from Horsforth.

Entering service in white, Enviro200 MMCs began to arrive on lease for service work as an upgrade to the previous Enviro200 type. SN16 OVP is seen arriving into Pudsey bus station blinded up ready for its return trip to Leeds.

Above and below: During summer 2020 it was announced that the Flying Tiger operation as part of Yorkshire Tiger, owned by Arriva, would be taken over by Transdev that September. Due to operational requirements, the existing operation was unable to recommence the Leeds to Airport 757 service part of the network, so CT Plus stepped in to bridge the gap for a few months. Two Enviro200s were obtained for this role and carried the 'Runway 757' branding for the very short time that this service was operated by them.

In summer 2020 CT Plus also gained a number of contracts in Huddersfield from TLC Travel. To operate these a yard was obtained in nearby Brighouse that was previously used by a closed independent. Ex-MCT MX12 DZG is seen arriving into Huddersfield bus station.

Seen returning from a Boston Spa school run with a reduced capacity of twenty is smartly presented SN55 BKZ. The white re-spray and masked LED blind is a far cry from the decommissioned Lothian livery a number of these entered service in.

For the launch of the Huddersfield services, CT Plus introduced line brands for their small range of services. Seen here at the terminus for the 'blue line' 374 route is YX65 RHJ.

On its way back to the Wakefield depot after operating a school run with a limited capacity of fifteen is Dennis Trident LR52 LTN. After three years of use by CT Plus in London red, this vehicle looked very neglected with replaced panels and a permanently masked-out destination blind.

With the amount of B7TL Geminis in use at this point, maintenance and parts replacement for this type was a major job. One of the 52-plated Geminis is seen in the Leeds depot being stripped for spares after withdrawal due to a major failure.

Once the closure of the Manchester Community Transport business took place, the Yorkshire business benefited from a number of extra relatively new Enviro200 MMC buses. Smartly presented YX19 ONS is seen in Pudsey on the 30 to Horsforth.

Once the Leeds Airport 757 service was handed back, the two Enviro200s obtained for this passed to Powell's Bus for use on their newly gained X20 service from Stagecoach. YX11 AEC is seen here arriving into Barnsley ready for another run to Doncaster.

Powell's Bus also became an official bus replacement provider for Stagecoach Supertram in 2020. Scania Omnicity double-decker 91 is seen by Crystal Peaks on a BL2 replacement run from Halfway to Sheffield on the blue line.

Due to teething issues with the Huddersfield operation, CT Plus sourced Fiat minibus 5104 to assist on the fleet and it remained until the closure. It is seen here operating 'blue line' route 375 to Dalton.

Parked at the exit to the Leeds depot before heading out on a school run is Volvo B7TL Gemini LF52 ZSP. CT Plus undertook rail replacement work for Northern Rail in their last few years of operation.

With a gap in the operation, Powell's Bus began operation of the now well-established 117 service between Rotherham and Bramley, passing through estates previously not served by public bus. YR59 NPD is seen leaving Rotherham.

When taking over the Powell's business, HCT Group gained a number of their Dennis Tridents sold to Powell's from the London operation. One example of these was PF52 TGZ, seen here passing Sheffield Interchange whilst on a tram replacement service.

Tram replacements were both long and short contracts, with a closure on the Yellow line from Sheffield to Middlewood taking place over Sundays in autumn 2020. For this contract, buses and drivers from Leeds were used, such as SN55 BKZ.

During evenings on the Yellow line replacement, Powell's Bus-based vehicles and staff were used to cover for Leeds drivers who were required for school services the next day. SN56 ABV, one of three ex-Lothian buses from Leeds, is seen at Middlewood.

Seen in Sheffield city centre on the city circular 10a service is Enviro200 YX11 AEC, having been displaced at this point on the X20 service and now seeing use on Sheffield locals.

Although most of the Enviro200 MMCs were branded up with CT Plus 'ivy', some missed out on this, such as SN16 OVO. It is seen here departing on the 'red line' 378 service to Mount.

Parked on Park Row in Leeds whilst operating an AccessBus contract with the P19 school service as a paper blind in the window is Optare Solo YJ09 LAE. This was one of the last of these repainted and upgraded by Metro, looking rather worn out until this point.

Looking very smart just after repaint and exhaust work by their owner Metro, a number of leased Optare Solos sit in Leeds depot in between AccessBus contracts.

One of the three ex-Lothian Geminis that were given to Powell's Bus upon purchase was SN56 ABV. It is seen here in unbranded state at Meadowhall at the end of an A1 service from Sheffield.

The CT Plus 'ivy' branding became a regular sight for customers on the Sheffield local services operated by Powell's Bus with all the Optare Solo SRs that entered service in full livery. One example, KX14 FHZ, is seen departing Hallamshire Hospital on a 10 service.

One of the last pre-CT Plus purchase double-deck buses with Powell's Bus was Volvo B7TL PJ52 LVX. This bus survived long enough to gain regional fleet number 2277 and is seen prior to operating an A1 service in Sheffield Interchange.

A short-term vehicle shortage at CT Plus at the start of 2021 saw the loan of two Enviro200s from the commercial fleet with HCT London. Carrying London number 302, MX14 FUT departs Sheffield Interchange on an A1 service to Meadowhall.

At times, vehicle loans and temporary transfers took place. However, with destination files varying at depots this sometimes led to incorrect blind files on buses being pushed into use, such as YX65 RHU, seen advertising the Leeds depot on a Huddersfield service.

During 2021 the number of withdrawn vehicles grew and changed position towards the fence. In this shot are withdrawn ex-Lothian and London Gemini examples and an ex-Powell's Bus coach that was placed up for sale but failed to find a buyer.

Nearly four years after the first example arrived, LF52 ZSO is seen in the depot looking very smart in the white re-spray with CT Plus names. This was one of very few painted out of London red with none of these ever carrying 'ivy' branding.

In summer 2021 route brands began to appear on Powell's Bus. The first of these was the 'Six' branding for route 6 between Sheffield, Hallamshire Hospital and Millhouses Tesco. Two Optare Solo SRs were painted, of which 1810 is seen here.

In a bit more of an 'action shot', 1810 is seen here again turning off Rockingham Street in Sheffield City Centre. The tight timings and traffic congestion on this service led to unreliability at peak times.

P3 WTL was one of two new to Reading Buses Scania Olympus buses purchased for Powell's Bus from Wheelers. These only lasted a few months before being sold on, with 2912 seen here on an A1 to Meadowhall. Note the old Reading Buses 859 number still present.

The second brand introduced by Powell's was the 'Zip' for the X20 service between Doncaster and Barnsley. Seen in the blue undercoat is Enviro200 MMC YX68 URG. This was its only trip out prior to receiving full route branding.

A random purchase to fulfil contract needs for the renewal of their Doncaster NHS Park & Ride contract was ex-Arriva London Wright Streetdeck SK68 TNJ. It is seen here in Sheffield on one of its first trips out, in use on staff training for a tram replacement.

Seen departing Doncaster Frenchgate with full 'Zip' branding is ADL Enviro200 MMC YX68 URG, one of two vehicles to receive this livery. The makeover was limited to an exterior repaint with the dealer stock interior layout unchanged.

Making its way around Furnival Gate roundabout after pausing in the city centre on a 10a to Manor Top via Hallamshire Hospital is Optare Solo YJ08 PFF. This was numbered 33 before gaining its four-digit fleet number and was initially new to Blackpool Transport.

Looking a little rough as it turns onto Flat Street to head into the Interchange is original Powell's Bus Dennis Trident AC02 POW, now numbered 2716. This was one of the final vehicles at Powell's Bus to be withdrawn before closure and was scrapped in summer 2022.

With buses operating short workings around, Optare Solo SR KX14 FJU powers down Arundel Gate as it prepares to attempt another 6 service to Millhouses. On this day abrupt heavy snow caused travel chaos, with Powell's services suspended shortly after this point.

Alongside services in Sheffield centre, Powell's also operated the Bradfield 61/62 services. Seen arriving in Hillsborough Interchange already blinded for another trip is KX14 FJU, the usual vehicle type choice for this semi-rural service.

With its rear axle flying higher than usual, Volvo B7TL Gemini SN55 BMU arrives into Sheffield Interchange for its break after operating a morning 060 school service. Note the Powell's fleet number still in place despite the CT Plus names.

Over summer 2021, CT Plus operated three vehicles for a brief period on a rail replacement job between Leeds and York. Seen here a few hours before the operator was taken off them is Volvo B7TL Gemini SN56 AFK at Leeds station.

Summer 2021 also saw First Bus suffer a driver shortage that led to CT Plus been offered work in Leeds to assist. Ex-Sheffield Community Transport Enviro200 MMC YX18 KNZ can be seen at The Springs on an X26 service operated on contract to First Bus.

Shortly into operating the X26/7 services on contract to First it became apparent that capacity was an issue. As a result, double-deckers began to be used, such as SN55 BPO, seen here leaving Leeds bus station.

A random arrival in 2021 for the Powell's business was midi Enviro200 MMC YX21 RRV. This was given the fleet number 1354 and operated primarily on Sheffield local work but also assisted on the 'Zip' X20 to cover longer members of type for repair.

Shortly before changes to traffic flows, MX12 DZF turns off Carver Street onto Wellington Street on a 6 towards the city centre. Since the photo was taken this road has been closed, with buses now turning onto Rockingham Street earlier.

After taking its lunch break in Sheffield Interchange, Dennis Trident PF52 TGZ is seen departing on its way to operate a school service 638 to Thurcroft to the east of the city. This vehicle was one of a number of ex-HCT London Tridents purchased by Powell's before the CT Plus buyout.

Despite having fleet names applied, LF52 ZPZ still adorned a rather tired-looking London red when seen here on Sovereign Street operating Leeds United shuttle service R2. CT Plus assisted on this contract due to a driver shortage at First Bus during 2021.

Seen on its way from Wisdoms Coaches bus works after repair is Wakefield-based Dennis Trident LR52 LTF. Note the two different school numbers in the window; it is presumed this bus operated both services back-to-back on a regular basis.

Despite its age, Volvo B7TL ALX400 V120 LGC looked very presentable operating Leeds United R2 shuttle service work on behalf of First Bus. Note the paper in the window explaining the hiring in set-up during this particular football game.

As the masses await shuttle buses for the Leeds United game, a selection of CT Plus buses arrive and depart with full loads of passengers. This scene shows the variety of presentation of vehicles at the time with a London red Gemini departing in the distance.

In summer 2021 CT Plus also operated Cocoon in the Park shuttle services once again to the festival at Temple Newsam. This particular year saw a reduced requirement for buses, with LF52 ZPR seen departing on the infrequent service that was operated.

As vehicle requirements kept adapting in 2021, buses were regularly changing depots. One-time Huddersfield-based ex-MCT Enviro200 MX12 DZG is seen by Leeds City Square after operating an 81 service from Pudsey.

Operation requirements sometimes meant that random vehicles would fill in temporarily on services. Seen here is a tired-looking Powell's-branded Enviro200 and a CT Plus-branded Volvo B7TL, seen between 11 and X26/7 duties in Leeds bus station.

CT Plus celebrated Pride during 2021 by branding up two vehicles to feature a pride rainbow on the 'ivy' livery. The single-deck chosen for this was SN16 OVP; the other vehicle to carry the rainbow branding was a Volvo B7TL Gemini new to Lothian.

Another photo of YY67 HBL, the Enviro200 with Powell's name, sees it in Pudsey bus station whilst operating the 30 service to Horsforth. During its time at Leeds depot this vehicle spent most of its service life using paper destination blinds.

Although ex-Lothian Geminis were preferred, the ex-London examples would sometimes appear on Leeds service work on contract to First. Seen leaving Seacroft bus station is LF52 ZSO, which was operating this 11 service 'top deck closed'.

Due to a major RTC that saw one of the original Optare Solo SR buses written off in Bradfield, YJ64 DWA arrived at Powell's Bus to fill the gap. The vehicle is seen departing on an A1 service to Meadowhall.

As Metro reduced the number of BMC Condors they owned and contracted to operators, a number of these were auctioned off. Seen leaving Manchester Shudehill during the Go North West strike was ex-CT Plus Yorkshire YJ56 ZTE.

Above and below: As fleet standardisation continued across the CT and Powell's network, more older vehicles were withdrawn. Seen parked withdrawn at the exit of the Leeds depot are old Powell's Bus BMC Condor 43 and Optare Solo 37. The BMC Condor had transferred from CT Plus upon the takeover with the Optare Solo purchased by Powell's Bus just before the sale took place. The withdrawal of the BMC Condors at Powell's saw the last new to Hull operation vehicles withdrawn from the fleet.

Also parked in the expanded withdrawn section of the depot was ex-HCT London Dennis Dart BX54 DLK, seen here surrounded by withdrawn Powell's vehicles.

As buses were replaced, a selection of random Enviro200 buses arrived to replace the vehicles. Enviro200 MX13 BAU was a very short-lived addition to the Powell's fleet, seen here operating the 5 service to Firth Park.

Although Solos were preferred, it also started to become common to see Enviro200s appear on the Bradfield circular services. At this point CT Plus veteran YX11 AEC is seen in Hillsborough Interchange awaiting its next circular.

As leased Enviro200s came and went, common vehicle shortages in the gaps saw some of the elderly school double-deckers appear on service. Volvo B7TL Plaxton President W452 WGH is seen at the Troydale turnaround on an 81 service to Leeds.

Despite some vehicles still looking unloved in the school fleet, nicely presented Volvo B7TL Gemini SN56 AHF departs the Interchange on an A1 to Meadowhall.

Optare Solo YJ55 BJO was one of the last remaining original Powell's Bus single-deck vehicles on fleet once the mass withdrawals took place, with it lasting until the closure. It is seen here arriving into Sheffield Interchange between duties.

Above and below: Towards the end of 2021, CT Plus was once again asked to assist First Bus in providing services on their behalf due to an ongoing driver shortage. This particular agreement saw them temporarily take over the 539 and 587 bus services in Halifax, using three newly acquired Enviro200 MMC midi-buses. These services were operated for a few months and then returned to First. At the time of writing, First Bus no longer operate either of these routes.

By this time numbered 1808 and with old Blackpool Transport 'Metro Coastliners' livery emerging at the front, YJ08 PFE is seen travelling along Arundel Gate on a 5 service.

Having been based at the Leeds depot for some time, Powell's-branded Enviro200 YY67 HBL was treated to destination repair and is seen arriving into Pudsey bus station on an 81 service. On the day of this photo this vehicle was operating without a ticket machine.

The start of 2022 saw disaster strike again and the withdrawn corner claim an extra vehicle in the form of Vamooz-branded X587 EGK. This Volvo B7TL was involved in a low bridge incident and would not see further use with CT Plus.

The last additions to the CT Plus Yorkshire operation before the closure were a small number of Volvo B9TL Gemini 2s that were based at the Leeds depot. LK59 CXA is seen arriving back at depot. These buses operated their entire time at CT Plus in this condition.

Seen racing along Arundel Gate is Scania Omnicity double-decker YR59 NPD. It was unusual to see Powell's double-deckers along this road; presumably this was being utilised on a driver changeover.

One final vehicle shortage at Powell's Bus saw CT Plus transfer over ex-London Dennis Trident 2709 to the fleet for primary use on school services. The vehicle is seen here with a single-strip LED blind operating the A1 service at Sheffield Business Park.

By 2022 PF52 TFX was the last of the ex-HCT London Dennis Tridents at Powell's purchased by them before the takeover. Featuring a 'thumpy' gearbox, 2721 is seen on the 3 service to Ravensfield.

Joining 2709 at Powell's Bus as a transfer from CT Plus was better-presented 2702 from Wakefield depot. This was one of a handful of London red buses ever treated to a re-spray. It is seen here leaving Sheffield Interchange on an A1 featuring a paper destination blind.

Once the Halifax work on contract to First was completed, the 71-plated Enviro200 MMC Midis were transferred to Wakefield depot for use on their Pontefract services. YX71 OJK is seen here running without a destination blind on the 39 service.

During the final weeks, the A1 service featured a mix of minibuses with double-deckers on set boards that rotated with school services. Optare Solo SR KX14 KJU is seen here at Catcliffe on a trip into Sheffield.

With paper school bus destinations in the window, AK02 POW powers through Sheffield Interchange during summer 2022 ready to start another trip on the A1 service.

The Powell's privately registered Dennis Tridents managed to make appearances until the end of the operation. Running with a paper blind, Parkgate Shopping-branded 2717 is seen on a 3 service bound for Rotherham.

After entering service in plain white, Optare Solo SR YJ64 DWA was treated to 'ivy' branding before the closure of the operation. It is seen here travelling down Rockingham Street on a 10 circular to Manor Top.

With branding for the Bristol Community Transport operation, Enviro200 YX65 RHU returned to Yorkshire from its long spell at Bristol just before the closure. It is seen in South Elmsall on the 39 service a week before the contract was lost to Globe Holidays.

Seen in the final week of operations was ex-Sheffield Community Transport Enviro200 MMC YX18 KNY, seen in Pontefract on the NHS Hospital Shuttle 113 service.

After much debate about the date of closure following an announcement on the Monday, Friday 8 August 2022 would be last day for CT Plus Yorkshire operations. On the morning, Optare Solo SR KX14 FJF is seen travelling down Brocco Bank on a 6 service.

Above and below: The last day saw a very limited service operate with bus drivers taking regular breaks in between scheduled trips due to the uncertainty of the situation. Taken at 11 a.m. on the last day, these photos show three vehicles parked around Sheffield Interchange that should have been operating the 5 and 10 services. As many of those who worked there did not turn up for work on this last day due to questions about getting paid, a very limited service operated on this final day in Sheffield.

The staff car for the day was Mercedes minibus GX64 EYY, seen here in Sheffield Interchange.

Seen parked at Meadowhall Interchange are two minibuses that operated the A1 on the last day, with no double-deck buses used in order to save money. The Optare Solo would be the author's last Powell's bus trip, with vehicles instructed to return to depot an hour after this photo was taken due to the threat of the gates being locked indefinitely.

Above and below: After the closure, the depots that were previously filled with buses began to be cleared, with buses returning to those that had leased them and being sold off for further use. By 9 September only B7TL Gemini LF52 ZTH was left in the Leeds depot for collection, this bus still retaining the Go Ahead London livery it arrived to the company in. Also, note the recruitment poster that was still present on the depot fence over a month after the closure. LF52 ZTH was removed shortly after these photos were taken.

By the following Monday, Stagecoach Yorkshire had taken over the Sheffield 6 service between the city centre and Millhouses. Holbrook-based ADL Enviro200 MMC 37606 is seen on an evening working on this service.

To respond to new school contract demand, Squarepeg purchased a small number of B7TLs from the recently closed Bournemouth Yellow Buses. Seen from the depot fence is HF03 ODW waiting for de-branding before entering service.

Above and below: To respond to new school contract demand, Leeds-based independent Tetley's turned away from their usual choice of Dennis Trident buses and towards B7TL buses to cover new service gains. Above is ALX400 LJ55 BSX, seen on delivery. This was one of three new to Arriva London vehicles to arrive from Stotts, Oldham. In addition, the company also gained two ex-CT Plus vehicles in the form of new to Lothian Geminis SN56 ABV and AFO. All vehicles were de-branded of previous operator lettering before commencing service.

One of two B7TL Gemini vehicles to be purchased by Hunters from the CT Plus Yorkshire fleet was LF52 ZTR, seen here having just been purchased and awaiting preparation into service. This was joined by LF52 ZRR, which had arrived in all-over white.

One bus that has lived a varied life is YJ07 EHR, new to First Leeds as their 53907. This bus, owned by Metro, spent most of its life with CT Plus as a spare AccessBus and has now transferred to TLC Travel for use on their public bus service work.

Above and below: Although many of the vehicles included in the auctions were eventually sold for further use, a number of the buses did not find buyers and were subsequently scrapped. Seen here in a storage yard pending transfer for scrap were three ex-CT Plus double-deckers, still carrying their fleet numbers on a mix of liveries that adorned them in service with the operator.

The October 2022 service changes saw some services reinstated from Powell's Bus that weren't initially taken on following the closure in August. Cawthorne's, an independent operator in Rotherham, took on two services in Sheffield following the closure and service 3 in Rotherham in October. For this service a variety of double-deck buses were used, as photographed, with vehicles rushed into service following purchase.

The October service changes also saw the Rotherham 117 service reinstated, a contract that Powell's had created themselves. TM Travel took on this service and used a variety of Optare Solos transferred from Trent Barton on this route.

Prior to contract changes in Derbyshire, Littles of Ilkeston obtained a number of the 67-plated Enviro200 MMC Midis to upgrade their fleet. CT Plus-branded SN67 XBJ is seen departing Alfreton bus station. These vehicles have since passed to Stotts, Oldham.

In Leeds, various independent operators stepped in to cover contracts with newly emerging operator Yorkshire Buses taking on the 61 service. An acquisition to the fleet was Dennis Dart MPD X511 WRG, seen here at John Charles Centre.

A surprise route takeover was the 30 service by school service dedicated operator A&A Coach Travel. Pleasantly presented ex-First Glasgow Volvo B7TL Plaxton President LK03 NHC is seen here at Pudsey bus station.

In Huddersfield, the community transport spirit continued to operate a number of the Huddersfield routes in the form of local independent South Pennine CT. Optare Solo Slimline YJ12 PNL is pictured arriving into Huddersfield bus station.

At the time of writing, the most recent CT Plus encounter was YX62 DHY, now number 31434 with Diamond Bus North West. Still operating in the base CT Plus Yorkshire white with Diamond Bus names, this bus entered service in January 2023.